In May of 1993, Rosemary Lewis, Bill Genshaw, and Julie Matthies came to the Clarkston Community Historical Society with a dream. They wanted to write a textbook on the history of Clarkston/Independence Township for the children in the Clarkston School District. Up to this point, the history of our community was taught only by some teachers throughout the district, and those teachers had no formal materials. They had to do their own research and then piece their program together as best they could. Rosemary Lewis was one of the teachers who struggled to do this. But she knew there was a better way. She contacted Bill Genshaw and Julie Matthies, and the textbook project began to develop.

When we in the Clarkston Historical Society heard about this textbook, we immediately knew that this was an important project. We felt that there would be few better ways to use our resources than this, and jumped at the opportunity to participate. We are proud to have provided the funding for both the creative work (by talented local artist Jim Russell) and the publishing of the book. We are also happy to have been able to provide research material, photographs, and other items which made writing the book a little easier for the authors. And we are pleased to know that, with our help, the children of Clarkston will know about the rich history of our community.

We would like to express our gratitude to all our members, many of whom provided photographs or information to the authors and artist, and we would like to congratulate the team on a job well done.

THE CLARKSTON COMMUNITY HISTORICAL SOCIETY BOARD OF DIRECTORS

Rae Anne Anderson
Jennifer Arkwright
Bill Basinger
Mary Alice Cook
Debbie DeVault
Kim Huttenlocher
Sharon Kingsbury
Dean Kudich
Jonathan Smith

ACKNOWLEDGEMENTS

Written with the coordinated efforts of:
Bill Genshaw, Ph.D
Rosemary Lewis
Julie Matthies

Edited By:
Kim Huttenlocher

Designed And Illustrated By:
James Russell

We'd like to thank the following organizations and individuals. Without their financial support, information, talents, and assistance, this book would have been more difficult to create.

Clarkston Board of Education
Clarkston Foundation
Clarkston Optimists
Ric and Mary Beth Huttenlocher
Charles Robertson
Toni Smith
George White

PHOTOGRAPHS AND HISTORICAL MATERIALS
Robert Beattie
Les Haight
Ethel Lynn Hyde
Robert McGowan
Gladys Porrit
Charles Robertson
Virginia Walters
Jane & Amanda Werner
George White
Ken Winship

Our Children's Heritage, A History of Clarkston/Independence Township. Copyright © 1995 Clarkston Community Historical Society. All rights reserved.

No part of this book may be used or reproduced in any manner without the written permission of the Clarkston Community Historical Society.

ISBN 0-9621749-1-2
ISBN 0-9621749-2-0

Our Children's Heritage

A History Of
Clarkston/Independence Township

This book is dedicated to the children of Clarkston. May you use the history of Clarkston to understand the present and preserve the uniqueness of our community for future generations.

ORIGINS

Around 1823, a man named Joseph Van Sycle came to Michigan from Independence, New Jersey. In honor of his hometown, he named the place you live in today Independence Township.

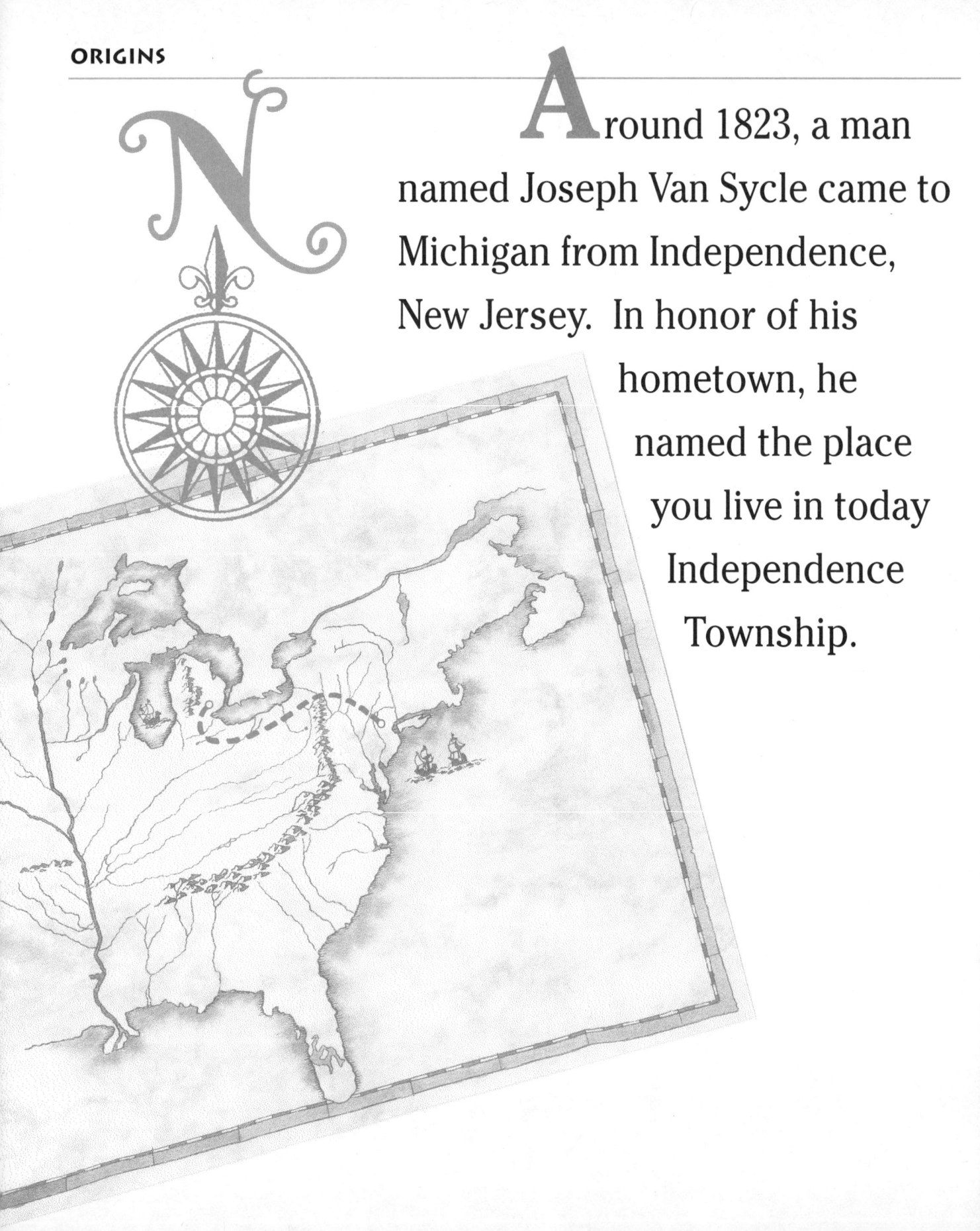

If you had traveled with Joseph to this area, it would have been very different from what you see today. There were no houses or stores as we see now.

The land was hilly and mostly covered with tall oak, pine, and elm trees. There were also flat parts of open land called plains.

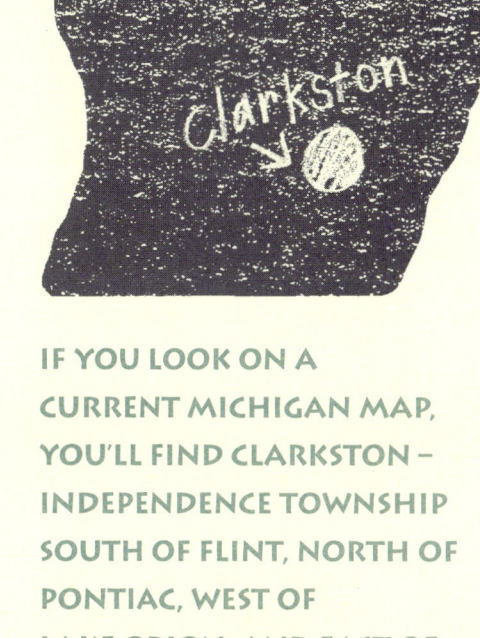

IF YOU LOOK ON A CURRENT MICHIGAN MAP, YOU'LL FIND CLARKSTON – INDEPENDENCE TOWNSHIP SOUTH OF FLINT, NORTH OF PONTIAC, WEST OF LAKE ORION, AND EAST OF WATERFORD.

GEOGRAPHY

Independence Township also had a lot of water. Fresh water was found in rivers, streams, lakes, and other wetland areas such as marshes and swamps. The large quantity of fresh water attracted many animals. Some of the animals that lived near these water areas were turkeys, wolves, bears, fish, deer, elk, turtles, snakes, birds, and muskrats.

INDIANS

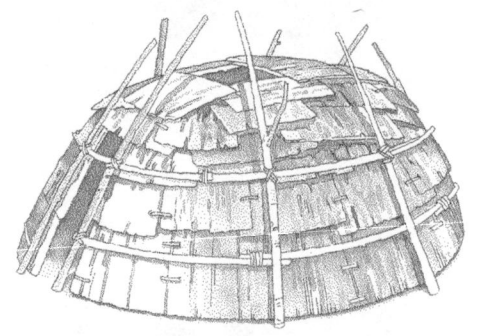

THE INDIANS BUILT THE WIGWAMS IN DIFFERENT SHAPES. THEY WERE EITHER CONE-SHAPED OR DOME-SHAPED.

When Joseph Van Sycle arrived in this area, he was greeted by people we call Native Americans, or Indians. The Indians were already living here in groups called tribes. Some of these tribes were named Wyandots, Sauks, Potawatame, Chippewa, and Ottawa. The Indians were called Woodlands Indians because they lived in the forest. They built their homes using long thin tree trunks and branches covered with tree bark. They were built to keep out the ice and snow. The Indians called these houses wigwams.

Usually one or more families lived in these homes. Their cooking and heat came from an open fire in the center of their home. The smoke from the fire escaped through a hole in the roof.

MANY BOWLS AND SPOONS USED FOR EATING WERE CARVED FROM WOOD WITH HANDLES IN THE SHAPE OF ANIMALS OR PEOPLE.

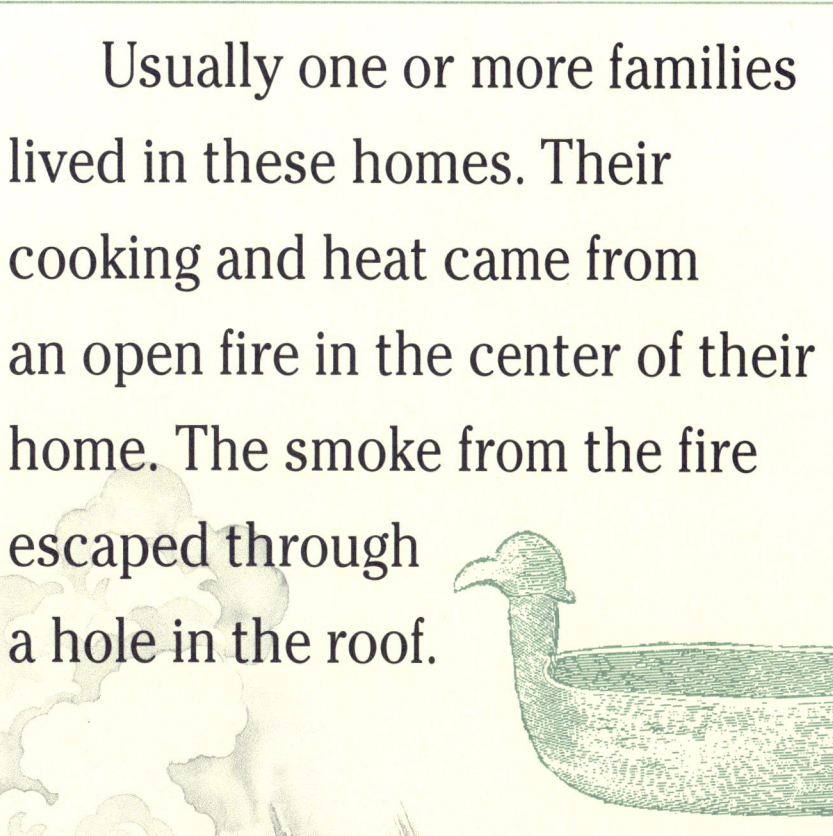

INDIANS

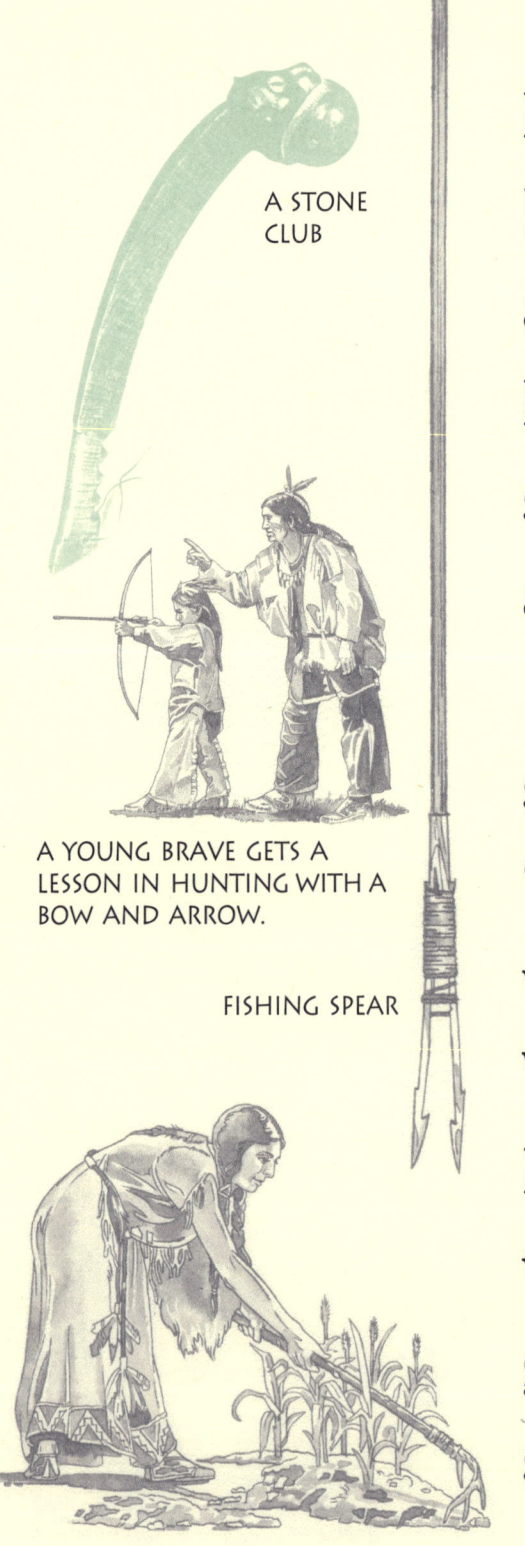

A STONE CLUB

A YOUNG BRAVE GETS A LESSON IN HUNTING WITH A BOW AND ARROW.

FISHING SPEAR

A STONE AXE USED TO HARVEST VEGETABLES.

Inside their homes the Indians used animal skins for beds and blankets. Animals were also hunted for food. The men hunted with bows, arrows, and stone clubs. They speared and netted fish.

In those days, the settlers called the men "braves," and the women were called "squaws." While the braves were out hunting, the squaws tended vegetable gardens. They grew pumpkins, corn, squash, and beans.

BLACK HUCKLEBERRY

WILD STRAWBERRY

HARVESTING WILD RICE

The women also gathered wild rice, nuts, and berries in the forest. In the spring, they collected sap from the maple trees to make syrup and sugar.

When there weren't enough animals to hunt and food to gather, the Indians had to move their village. Often their new village was not far from the old village. They built new homes and planted new gardens.

CHIEF SASHABAW

The plains area of Clarkston–Independence Township was home to Chief Sashabaw. He belonged to one of the southeastern Michigan tribes. The plains were a hunting and fishing ground for the Indians. Because the soil on the plains was fertile, they also used it for farming.

CHIEF SASHABAW TREASURED THIS BEAUTIFUL LAND. THEREFORE, HE GAVE HIS NAME TO THE SMALL WANDERING STREAM AND THE LOVELY PLAINS. THIS AREA IS LOCATED NEAR NORTH SASHABAW ELEMENTARY SCHOOL.

Chief Sashabaw developed a special friendship with a white settler named Oliver Williams. The two men treated each other as brothers. They helped each other and worked well together. The children of Oliver Williams, Mary and Oliver, played with the Indian children. Mary and Oliver were given Indian names by the Chief as a symbol of his friendship.

Sometime before 1834, Chief Sashabaw became very ill and died. He was buried near Oliver Williams' home on the banks of Silver Lake, in Waterford Township.

AN INDIAN STORY

This story is about Chief Sashabaw's half-brother Wa-me-gan. Wa-me-gan was big, strong, and brave. Danger did not frighten him.

One cold winter day while Wa-me-gan was hunting in the forest, he met a huge bear. The bear looked very angry and mean, but Wa-me-gan was not afraid. He knew the bear would provide much meat for his family. The brave used his rifle to fire one shot at the bear. However, the shot was not enough to kill such a huge bear.

Determined to kill it, Wa-me-gan charged with his knife, but the bear was too strong. When Wa-me-gan did not return from the forest after several days, his sons Ke-o-qum, Mashquet, and As-a-gum began to search for their father.

THE DRIFTING SNOW MADE IT DIFFICULT TO FOLLOW WA-ME-GAN'S TRACKS.

After searching day and night, Wa-me-gan was found lifeless against a tree. He had died from injuries he received from the bear. Angry and hurt by the loss of their father, Ke-o-qum, Mashquet, and As-a-gum sought and killed the bear. They brought the bear back to their village and used the meat to feed them for the winter.

WHAT HAPPENED TO THE INDIANS

The Indians remained in this area for a while after Chief Sashabaw died. However, as more white settlers moved to Clarkston–Independence Township, the Indians were not able to live as they had lived in the past. The white settlers took the Indians' hunting grounds for farmland. Many Indians were forced to move to the central part of the United States.

THE INDIANS CARRIED THEIR BELONGINGS ON A TRAVOIS PULLED BY A HORSE OR DOG. THE TRAVOIS WAS MADE WITH TWO LONG POLES AND A PLATFORM OR NET.

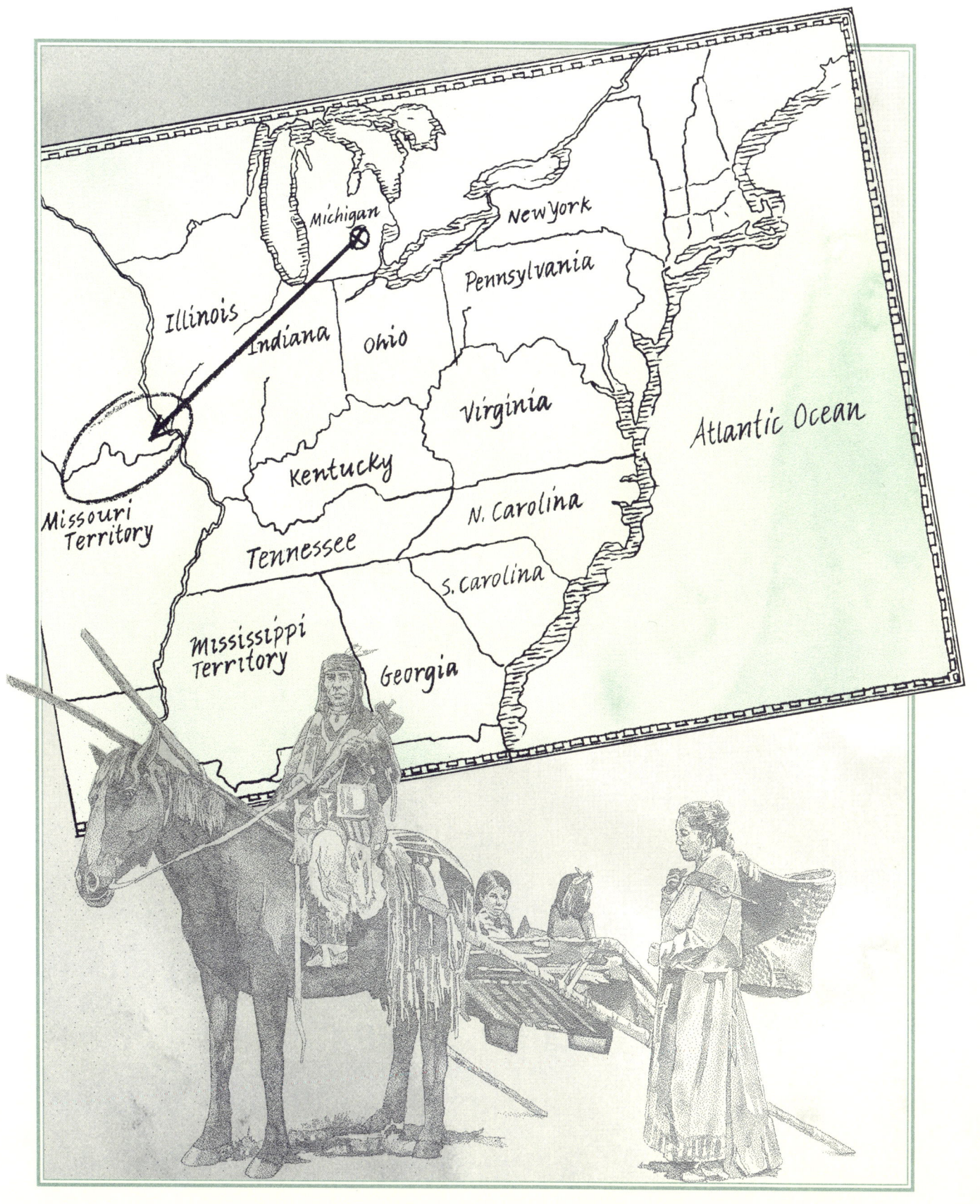

THE FIRST SETTLERS

The first white settlers came to Independence Township in 1823. There were no roads, only Indian trails. The early settlers traveled through forests, swamps, marshes, and over fallen trees. Often while traveling through swamps and marshes, the women and children had to be carried on the men's backs.

The first people settled in the Sashabaw Plains area and on the land where the city of Clarkston is located. Remember that this area was not yet known as Clarkston.

THE FIRST SETTLERS

Independence is a township. A township is a large area of land that includes houses, farms, and roads. This area is often six miles on each side which means the whole area is thirty-six square miles. Usually, a township has its own government which could include a mayor or supervisor. The mayor or a supervisor would help to make laws for the township.

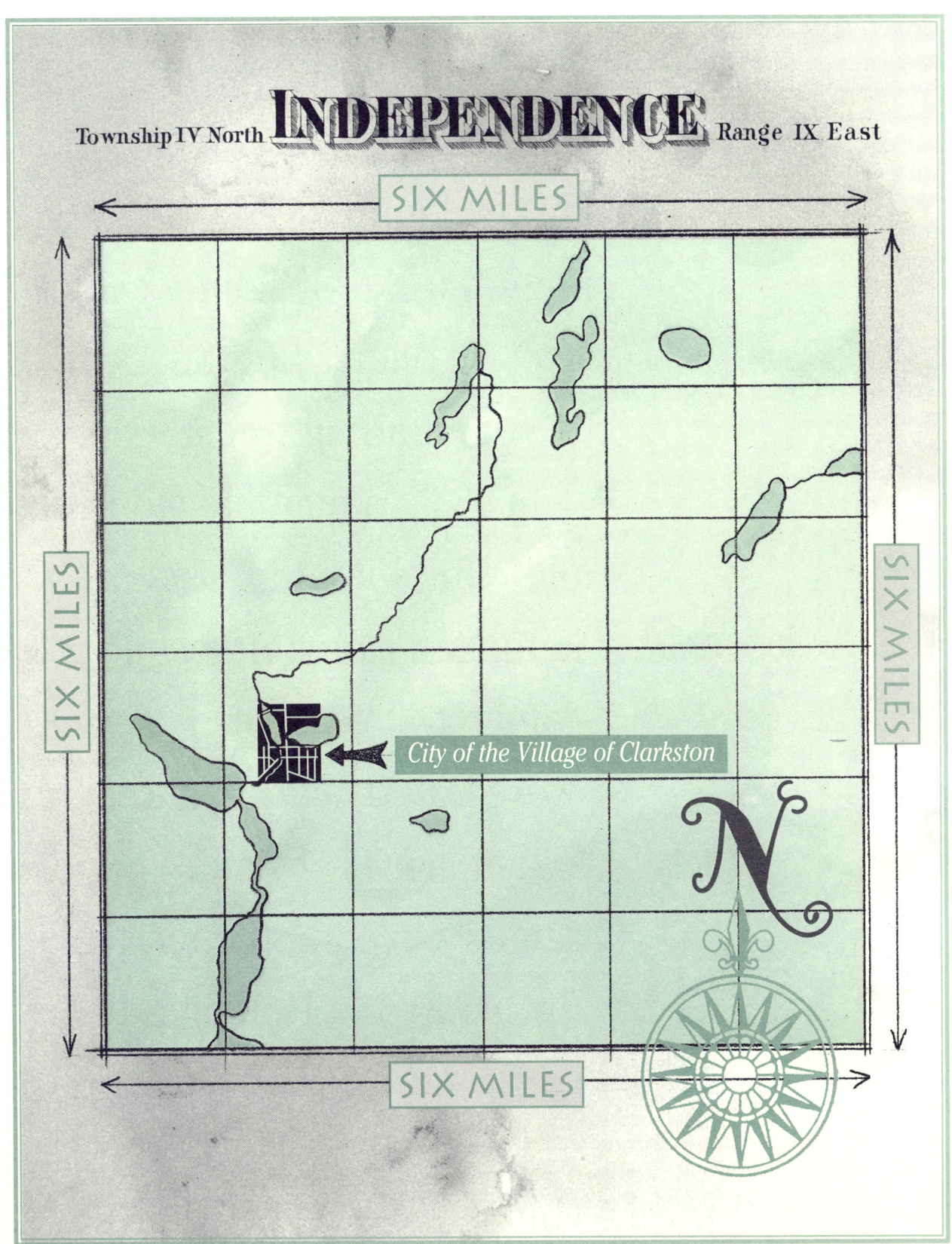

BEGINNINGS OF CLARKSTON

The first house in Independence Township was built by Linus Jacox, in 1830. He built it out of skinny cedar logs. He planted potatoes among the surrounding trees.

In 1832, a man named Butler Holcomb bought Mr. Jacox's land. Mr. Holcomb brought his family to live here. His sons were David, age 15, and William, age 8. As more people came to live in Independence Township, Mr. Holcomb helped to organize a town.

He built a saw mill, which cut trees into boards so people could build houses. He was so helpful and so important to the town that Holcomb Street was named after him and his family.

As more people moved to Independence Township, the area we now know as The City of the Village of Clarkston became a central place where people would meet to talk. They shopped in the stores and attended church and school. It was then that this central area was given the name Clarkston.

FOUNDING FATHERS

Clarkston was named after two brothers, Jeremiah and Nelson Clark. Jeremiah arrived from New York in 1832. Nelson heard from Jeremiah that the new area he had moved to was a wonderful place to live, so Nelson joined Jeremiah in 1836.

Two years later the brothers bought the saw mill which had been built earlier by Butler Holcomb near the Mill Pond.

HOME OF NELSON CLARK, ON NORTH MAIN STREET. BUILT IN 1855.

JEREMIAH CLARK

EDWIN G. CLARK – ELDEST SON OF JEREMIAH CLARK.

EDWIN CLARK'S FARM STILL EXISTS TODAY ON ALLEN ROAD. IT IS NOW CALLED BITTERSWEET FARM.

THE CLARKSTON MILLS

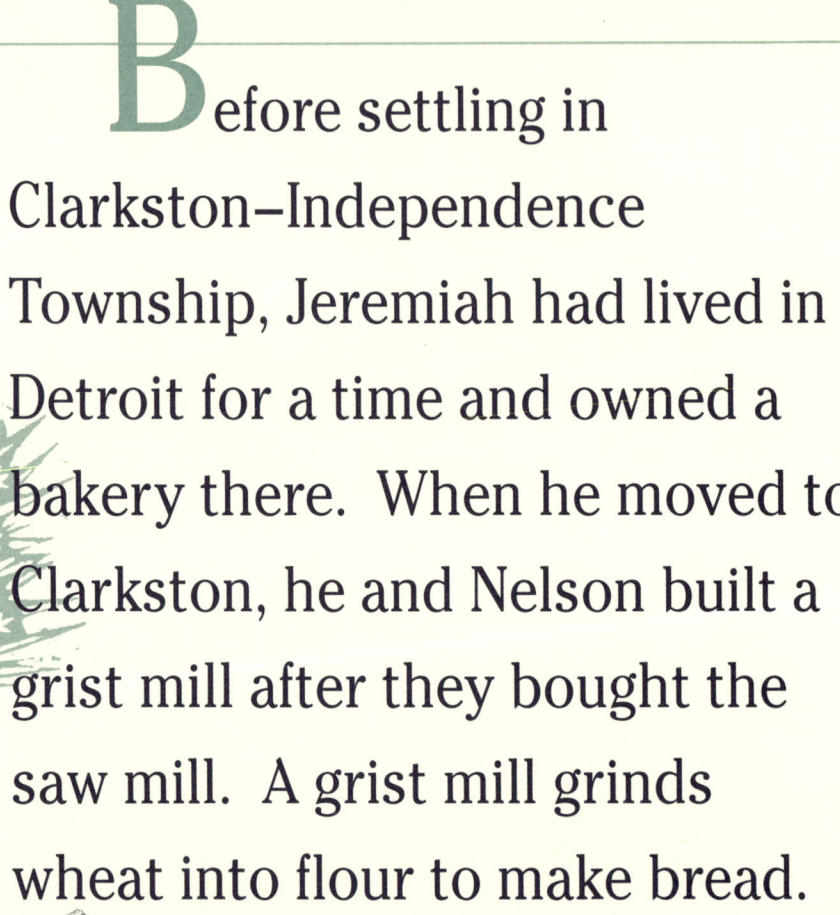

Before settling in Clarkston–Independence Township, Jeremiah had lived in Detroit for a time and owned a bakery there. When he moved to Clarkston, he and Nelson built a grist mill after they bought the saw mill. A grist mill grinds wheat into flour to make bread.

The Clark brothers knew that the settlers would need both wood for their homes and flour to make bread to eat.

REAR VIEW OF THE ORIGINAL CLARKSTON MILLS, LOOKING NORTH FROM DEPOT STREET.

THE GRISTMILL WAS DRIVEN BY A LARGE PADDLE WHEEL.

VILLAGERS NAME CLARKSTON

The Clark family worked to improve the small village that was being settled. They planted the first apple trees, which they had brought from New York. They built a fish hatchery stocked with brook trout, opened a general store, and acted as postmasters.

Because of all the things they did to help the town, the settlers of this area held the Clark brothers in high esteem. The people were grateful for what the Clark brothers had done. In 1842, they voted to name the village Clarkston.

MAILMAN – ELMER VLIET C 1910, IN FRONT OF THE DEMAREST HOUSE.

EARLY TRANSPORTATION

If you had walked through the Village of Clarkston when Jeremiah and Nelson Clark lived here, you would have walked on dirt roads. When it rained, it was muddy. These muddy roads made traveling difficult.

Traveling in the village and township was done by foot and on horseback. Wagons and carriages pulled by horses or oxen were also used. But soon, the people needed a better way to transport supplies and people to this area. They decided to build a railroad.

VIEWING INTERSECTION OF MAIN STREET AND WASHINGTON, LOOKING WEST ON WASHINGTON STREET

HUCKLEBERRY RAILROAD

In 1851, the first railroad was built near Independence Township. This made traveling faster and easier. Many people living in cities came to Clarkston because it was in the country. Cities, like Detroit and Pontiac, were noisy, hot and dirty. People came to Clarkston–Independence Township for vacations. Here they could fish, swim, and walk in the woods.

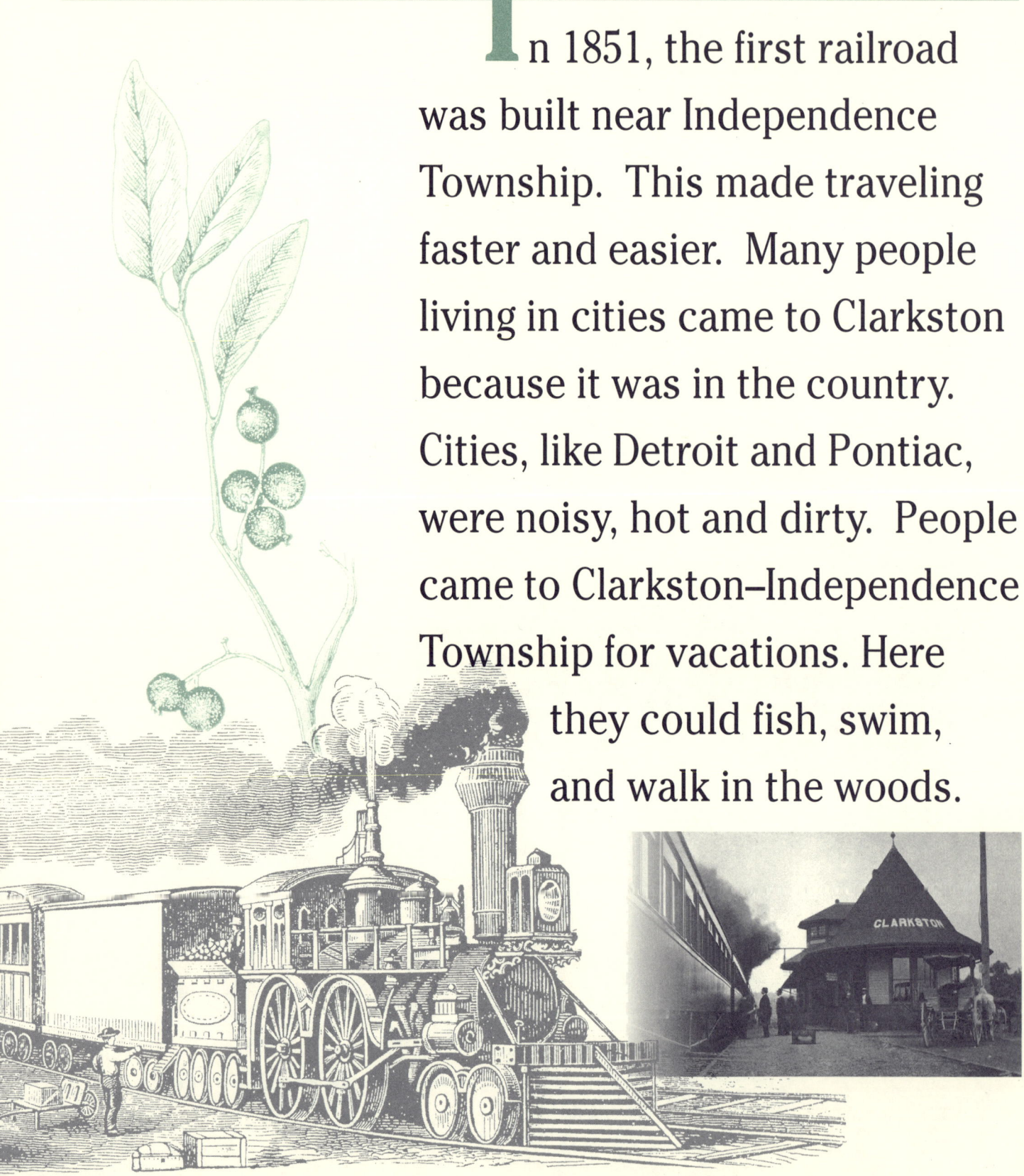

As they traveled through the area, they may have stayed at the Demarest or Deer Lake Inns. Travelers could sleep and eat at these inns.

The railroad was nicknamed "The Huckleberry Line" because it moved so slowly that passengers could jump off, pick huckleberries, and jump back on the last car of the train.

DEER LAKE INN

DEMAREST HOUSE

EARLY BUSINESS COMMUNITY

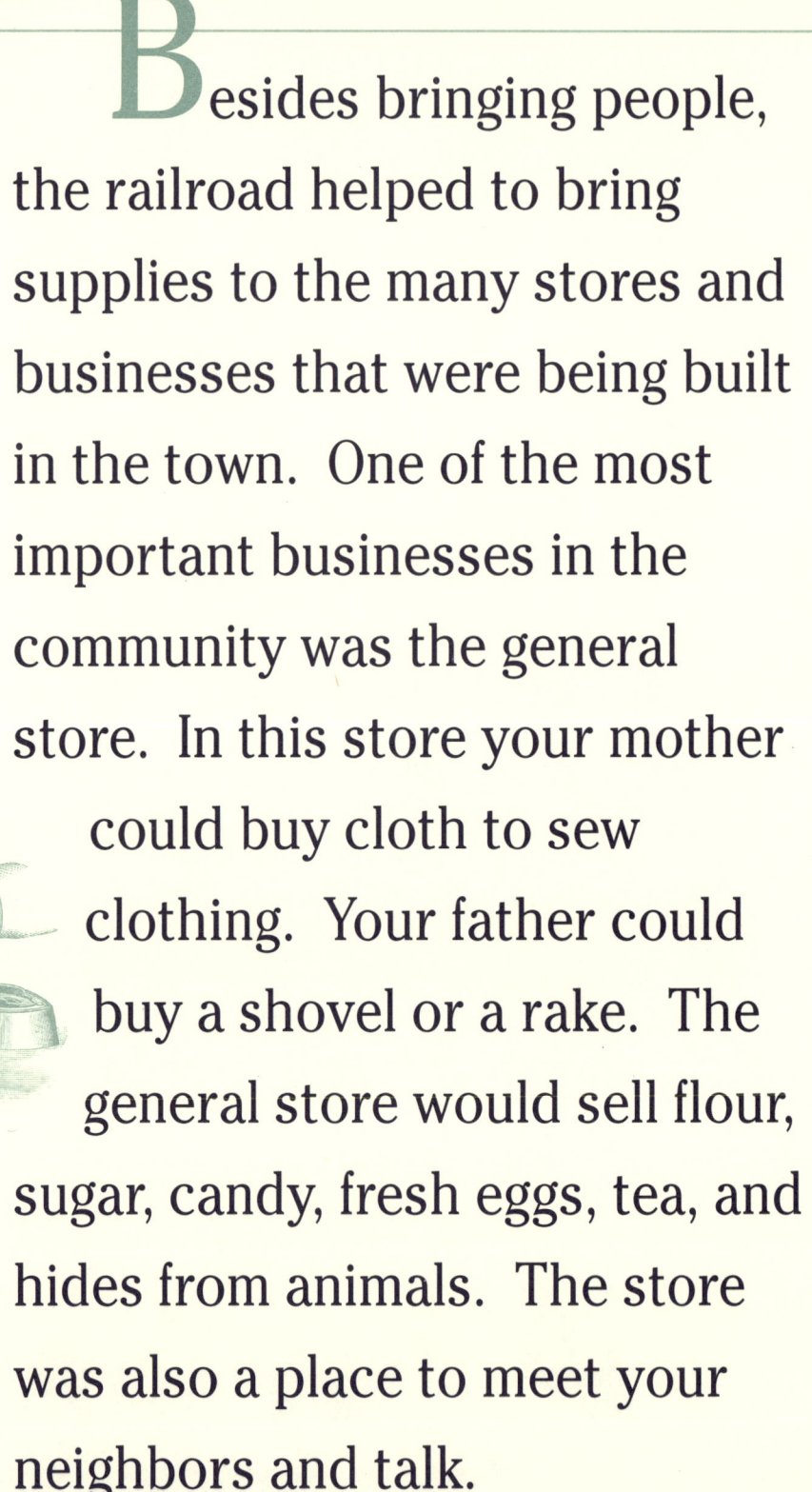

Besides bringing people, the railroad helped to bring supplies to the many stores and businesses that were being built in the town. One of the most important businesses in the community was the general store. In this store your mother could buy cloth to sew clothing. Your father could buy a shovel or a rake. The general store would sell flour, sugar, candy, fresh eggs, tea, and hides from animals. The store was also a place to meet your neighbors and talk.

IN THE EARLY DAYS OF CLARKSTON, A SHOEMAKER WAS CALLED A COBBLER.

Another important business person in town was the shoemaker. A shoemaker would make and sell shoes for everyone in the family. Shoes were expensive and you would probably own only one pair a year. Each child took a turn having his or her foot traced on leather. Several weeks later, the shoemaker would return with your shoes. The first shoes were styled like Indian mocassins.

EARLY BUSINESS COMMUNITY

If you lived in Clarkston–Independence Township back then, you would see that almost everything was very different than it is today. You would not have had as many clothes as you have now. Your clothes had to be made by your mother or a tailor.

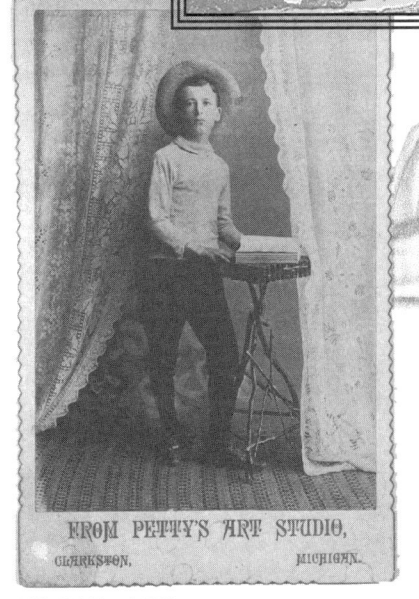

LEE CLARK C 1892

Often, the girls wore long dresses and high boots even to do chores in the barn. The boys wore short pants and high socks. Toys were different. Mothers made rag dolls for their children out of old dresses and shirts. Fathers made wooden boats or trains for their children. Since television and radio had not been invented, families sang songs, read books, and told stories at night.

EARLY BUSINESS COMMUNITY

Even your home might have been different. It could have been made from stones and logs instead of bricks or boards. Some of the houses built long ago are still here today. You can see many of them if you walk down Main Street or Holcomb Street.

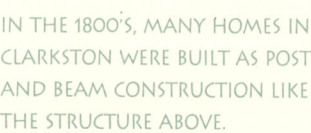

IN THE 1800'S, MANY HOMES IN CLARKSTON WERE BUILT AS POST AND BEAM CONSTRUCTION LIKE THE STRUCTURE ABOVE.

42

Just like in your home, furniture was either built by your family or bought from the town's furniture store.

FROM INDIAN PATH TO BUSY SUPERHIGHWAY

There were many Indian paths that settlers used to travel in Michigan. These paths did not destroy nature but were found winding around trees, lakes, and swamps. One path that was used for many years was called the Saginaw Trail. The Indians used this worn path on their journeys from Detroit to Saginaw. As more and more people began to use the Saginaw Trail, it became necessary to make the path wider. Settlers traveled first on foot, then by horseback and wagon, and finally by automobile. The early Indian paths became roads.

The Saginaw Trail was one of the paths that became a road. This path became Dixie Highway. In 1920, Dixie Highway became a paved road. It took more than a year to pave the gravel road in Independence Township.

EARLY ROAD WORKING MACHINERY

As more roads were paved, people could move from big cities like Pontiac and Detroit to villages and towns like Clarkston. As automobiles became heavier and more powerful, people were able to travel longer distances at faster speeds.

THIS OLD GAS STATION FROM THE 1920'S, STILL EXISTS AT THE CORNER OF MAIN STREET AND CLARKSTON ROAD.

The roads could not handle the amount of traffic and the new high speed of the cars.

FROM INDIAN PATH TO BUSY SUPERHIGHWAY

AS WORKERS DUG UP THE GROUND TO BUILD ADDITIONAL LANES, AN ARCHEOLOGIST FOUND BURIED ARROW HEADS AND POTTERY THERE. THESE ARTIFACTS WERE TREASURES TO SAVE, AND CAN NOW BE SEEN IN LOCAL MUSEUMS.

In 1956, the State of Michigan received money from the Federal Government to build super highways. This included I-75 and I-94

In 1962, I-75 passed through Independence Township. I-75 brought many changes to the Clarkston–Independence area. More people moved to the village and township. More houses and schools were built.

After many years, there were even more cars traveling on Dixie Highway, and it became necessary to make it wider.

In 1986, they widened it to five lanes.

MAJOR EVENTS

A JOURNALIST WRITES STORIES FOR THE NEWSPAPER.

MOST SMALL NEWSPAPERS WERE PRINTED ON A PRINTING PRESS LIKE THIS, CALLED A WEB PRESS.

As Clarkston–Independence Township grew, people needed a way to find out what was happening in the area. They needed a way to tell everyone when the circus was coming to town, which family just had a new baby, or who was running in the elections for the Village Council or the Clarkston School Board. The people decided that a newspaper was the best way to do this. Starting about 1929, the newspaper was called the *Clarkston News*.

We can still read it today.

SOMETIMES, BOYS WERE HIRED TO DELIVER THE NEWSPAPER TO THE LOCAL PEOPLE.

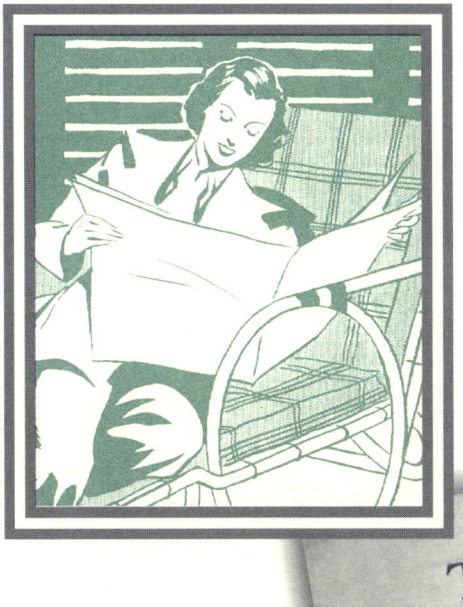

Over the years, the *Clarkston News* has written stories about big events that changed Clarkston–Independence Township. Here are three of those stories: one about a bank robbery, one about a flood, and one about a fire.

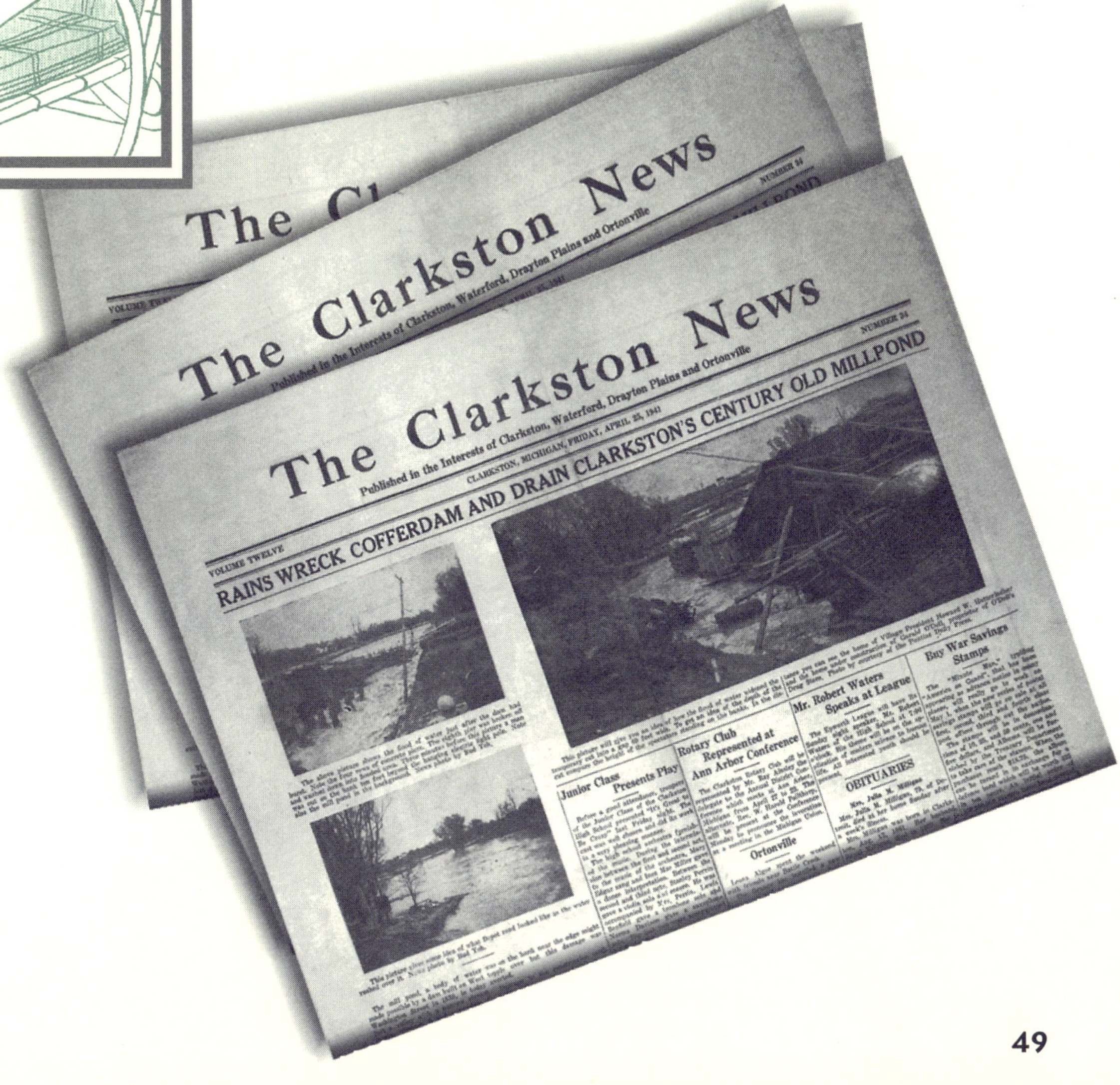

The Clarkston News

Published in the Interests of Clarkston, Waterford, Drayton Plains and Ortonville

VOLUME TWELVE — CLARKSTON, MICHIGAN, FRIDAY, APRIL 25, 1941 — NUMBER 24

RAINS WRECK COFFERDAM AND DRAIN CLARKSTON'S CENTURY OLD MILLPOND

Junior Class Presents Play

Rotary Club Represented at Ann Arbor Conference

Mr. Robert Waters Speaks at League

Buy War Savings Stamps

OBITUARIES

Ortonville

THE 1932 BANK ROBBERY

On July 16, 1932, a summer day in Clarkston, the people of the village knew something was very wrong. They heard the bank's burglar alarm blaring and the blasting of guns. The bank was being robbed.

The three robbers stole money from the bank and sped away in a 1932 Chevrolet. They seemed to disappear. The police could not find them. The bandits drove into a hidden area off Waldon Road and left the 1932 Chevrolet.

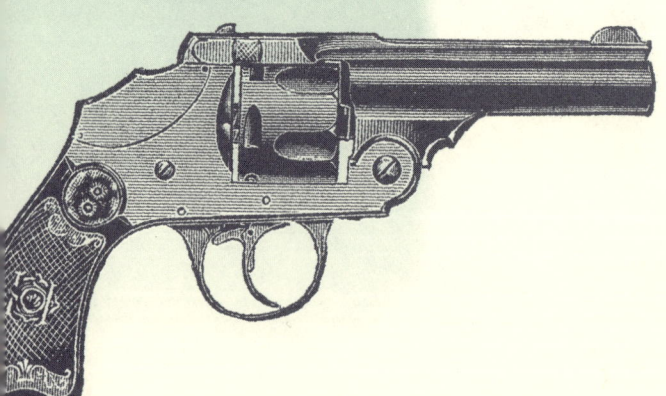

THE 1932 BANK ROBBERY

The robbers changed their clothes so they looked like farmers. Then they drove off in a Model A Ford to a farm in northern Lapeer. They thought no one would be able to find them.

The robbers were careless. A young boy, who lived on a farm next to the bandits in Lapeer, found out about the robbery. The bandits were afraid he would tell the police, so they forced him to join them in their next robbery.

The young boy knew that robbing a bank was wrong. He decided to report it to the bank manager. The manager told the police. The police raced to the farmhouse to arrest the robbers.

When they arrived at the farm, the police burst through the front and back doors.

Guns were fired as the police entered. In the shoot-out, one policeman and one bandit were killed. Another policeman was wounded. He later died. The other two robbers were caught and sent to prison.

THE 1932 BANK ROBBERY

*** The bandits didn't scoff at small change, taking seven rolls of pennies with them.

Dude DeMond had to shave using both hands on the razor after all the excitement Saturday night.
***

REPORTS FROM RESIDENTS ABOUT THE ROBBERY TAKEN FROM THE CLARKSTON NEWS, JULY 22, 1932.

After the bandits were arrested, the police had to find the money that was stolen. The bandits had hidden the money in a very safe place. The stolen money was found hidden in a manure pile on the farm. The money was returned to the Clarkston bank.

Lee Clark saw the bandits turn the corner by the Vulcan Plant and said that they were going so fast that they went around that corner on two wheels and very nearly tipped over.
***

Monday morning saw a gun salesman in town, visiting the bank and several stores.
***

THE NIGHT THE DAM WENT OUT

During World War II many of the countries in the world fought each other over land.

Some countries wanted more land than they had. The United States and other countries fought to stop them.

In 1942, many of the newspaper stories in Clarkston were about World War II. The war took place very far away in Europe. Young men and women from Clarkston joined the army and went away to fight. The newspaper kept their families and friends informed about what was happening to them.

MANY WOMEN WENT TO WORK IN FACTORIES WHILE THE MEN WERE AWAY FIGHTING IN THE WAR.

MEN AND WOMEN FROM CLARKSTON/INDEPENDENCE TOWNSHIP WHO FOUGHT IN WORLD WAR II, WERE LISTED ON A LARGE SIGN THAT WAS DISPLAYED IN THE CENTER OF TOWN.

THE NIGHT THE DAM WENT OUT

During the war, a man named Henry Ford visited Clarkston. He was looking for a place to build a factory. He needed a factory to help build tank parts which were used in the war. He saw that Clarkston had a Mill Pond. A mill pond is a body of water that can be used to provide power to run a factory. Before he could use the Mill Pond, Henry Ford had to clean some of the mud and weeds from the pond. This would cause the water to move more quickly and provide more power. To do this, he built a temporary dam made of boards and dirt, so he could make a permanent dam.

THE NIGHT THE DAM WENT OUT

The trouble started one night when there was a heavy rainstorm. The temporary dam was too weak to hold back all the extra water. This caused the dam to break. The water flooded the land all the way to Pontiac.

HENRY FORD BUILT A WOODEN ROAD ALONG THE EDGE OF THE MILL POND SO TRACTORS AND TRUCKS WOULD NOT SINK INTO THE MUD.

The flooding made the land very soft. Tractors and trucks were used to clean and carry out the mud and muck from the Mill Pond. The mud and muck were given to the Clarkston people to add to their soil. This made the soil better for growing crops and other plants.

A FIRE THAT CHANGED DOWNTOWN CLARKSTON

Firemen Battle Blaze in Clarkston Landmark

When the dam broke and water flooded all of Clarkston, there were pictures and stories in the Clarkston News. Other events that the Clarkston News wrote about were fires. Fires are very dangerous. They can destroy buildings and harm people and animals.

There have been many fires in the Clarkston–Independence area. As buildings were burned down, the Clarkston area changed in the way it looked.

One of these fires took place in 1944. In the village there was a Ford automobile dealership known as Beattie's Garage.

It was located on Main Street at the southwest corner of Depot Road. Beattie's sold and repaired cars.

One evening a small fire started inside the garage. When the fireman arrived, they could not open the door because it was locked. Mr. Beattie told the firemen that they could break down the door.

A FIRE THAT CHANGED DOWNTOWN

The firemen wanted to have their water hoses ready before they went inside the building.

In 1944, many fire trucks did not carry water. The firemen used large hoses to pump water from streams and lakes. In order for the firemen to fight the fire at Beattie's Garage, they had to stretch the hose from the Clinton River in Depot Park to the garage.

Somehow, the hose became tangled and the water could not flow through the hose. While the firemen were trying to untangle the hose, the fire grew larger.

Inside the garage, Mr. Beattie had stored large drums of alcohol. Alcohol burns easily, like gasoline. So, when the fire spread to the drums of alcohol, they exploded!

By the time the firemen had untangled the hose, the building was completely in flames. The fire got so hot it caused the water to boil. The Ford Dealership was destroyed. Mr. Beattie rebuilt his garage at a new location on Dixie Highway.

CHANGES IN OUR COMMUNITY (1950 – PRESENT)

TOP PICTURE, FROM LEFT:
GARY ROBERTSON, KAY ROBINSON,
TOM BULLEN, JIM COLLINS, AND
CHARLIE ROBERTSON.
DRAWING WITH CHALK.

The best way to find out about changes that have happened in Clarkston–Independence Township is to talk to someone who has lived here all of his or her life. Charlie Robertson was born in the Village of Clarkston and grew up here. He can remember when things looked very different than they do now. When he was a little boy, he and his friends used to play in the woods and open fields. Mr. Robertson said, "Most of the fields and woods where my friends and I often went hiking, camping, and hunting are now filled with houses."

CHILDREN'S ACTIVITIES

KIDS PLAYING ON ROBERTSON COURT.
FROM LEFT:
JIM COLLINS, MIKE THAYER,
GARY ROBERTSON, AND
CHARLIE ROBERTSON. 1942

When Mr. Robertson was a little boy, children used to play outside more often because there were no televisions, computers, or video games. In the wintertime, boys and girls would ice skate on the Mill Pond, and Depot Road was used for sledding. There were not as many cars back then, so it was safe to sled on the street. (It would not be safe today.)

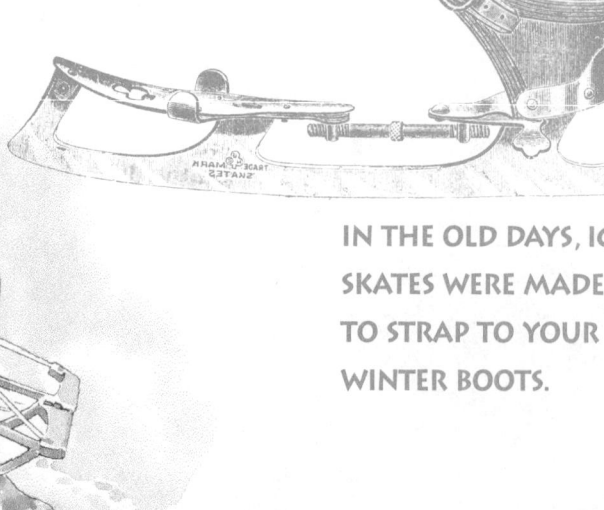

IN THE OLD DAYS, ICE SKATES WERE MADE TO STRAP TO YOUR WINTER BOOTS.

In the summer, the children swam in the lakes and ponds. They played marbles and baseball. They also enjoyed football, basketball, jump rope, hopscotch, and ball and jack games. The boys and girls often used their imaginations to make up new and exciting games.

IN THE 1920'S, KIDS COULD CAMP AND FISH WITH THEIR FAMILIES AT ED HAIGHT'S CAMP SITE ON CEMETERY LAKE.

FARMING

When Clarkston was first settled, many people who lived here were farmers. They grew crops like wheat, potatoes, and apples. The crops were sold to people who lived in cities like Pontiac and Detroit where there were no farms. They also sold milk from cows, eggs from chickens, and wool from sheep.

NELSON MORGAN'S BARN RAISING.
JUNE 30, 1915

LAND USE CHANGES

As more and more people moved into Clarkston, the land was needed for houses. Farmers sold their land, and the people who bought it built houses and apartments. Some of the land became subdivisions of houses. Subdivisions have lots of streets, and the houses are built next to each other. Some subdivisions have hundreds of houses. Later, other open areas were used for building condominiums and modular houses, and creating parks.

PARKS

As houses were built on many of the wooded areas and open fields, people needed places to walk, run, swim, play sports and games. Land was set aside by Independence Township and the Village of Clarkston to be used as parks. Parks like Clintonwood, Independence Oaks, and Depot Park are used as play areas today. These parks have been opened for families to enjoy picnics and other outdoor activities.

Clintonwood Park has baseball diamonds, basketball hoops and volleyball courts. You can rent a boat or swim at Independence Oaks. At Depot Park, children can play on playground equipment.

SCHOOLS

Schools in our community have gone through many changes. The early schools in Clarkston and Independence Township were one room school houses. All the children, no matter what grade they were in, were taught in one room by one teacher. This worked very well when there were only a few children who lived in the area. But as more people came to live here, bigger schools and more teachers were needed.

SCHOOLS

YOU CAN STILL SEE THE FIRST BIG CLARKSTON SCHOOL BUILT ON MAIN STREET. IT IS NOW THE INDEPENDENCE TOWNSHIP HALL.

BELOW, THE SCHOOL ON EAST CHURCH STREET REPLACED THE MAIN STREET SCHOOL FOR ALL GRADES.

A large school was built on Main Street in 1912. It was a school for children in kindergarten through twelfth grade. That school was more like our schools are today, except that all the children in Clarkston fit into only one school! Today there are six elementary schools, two middle schools, and one high school in our community. Many children attend these schools.

BUSINESSES

Businesses in Clarkston-Independence have changed along with everything else in our community. Businesses had to change as the needs of the people who lived here changed.

When people used horses and wagons to get from place to place, there were blacksmith shops and feed stores. Today, because most people drive cars, there are auto repair garages.

When traveling by horse and wagon to get from place to place, people moved much more slowly than we do in our cars.

BUSINESSES

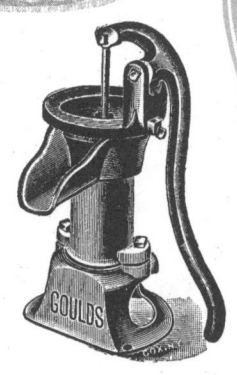

THE GENERAL STORE IN CLARKSTON WAS WALTER'S GENERAL STORE. TODAY, YOU CAN STILL SEE THAT BUILDING AT 5 SOUTH MAIN STREET.

This was especially true in the winter when it was cold and the roads were covered with snow. Since it was harder to get to places, most small towns like Clarkston had a general store. It was a place where you could buy food, clothes, toys, tools, and books. Everything you needed was in one spot.

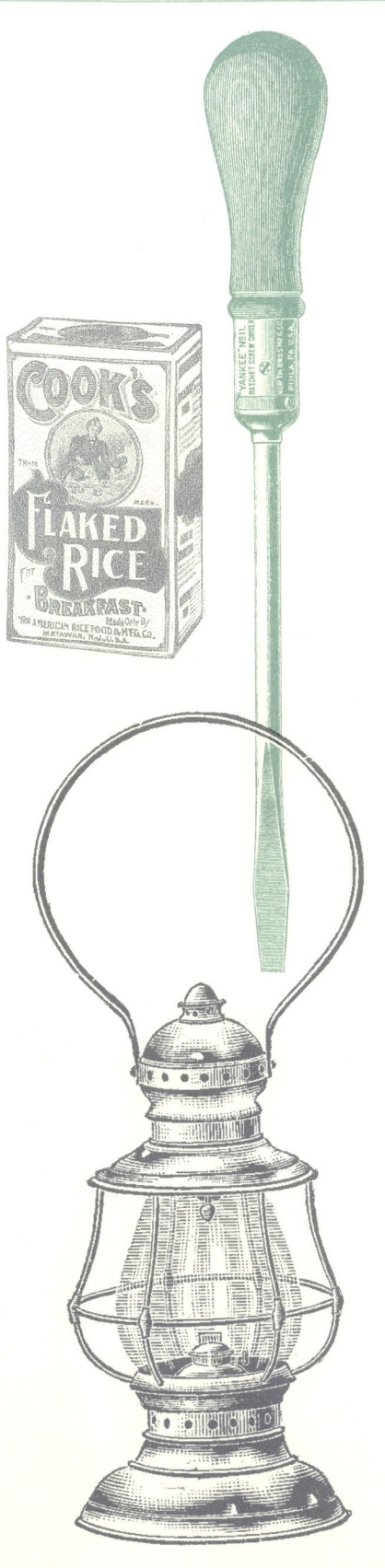

Now, because we have cars and paved roads, we can go to many different places to buy the things we need. We buy cereal and milk for our breakfast at a supermarket or grocery store. We buy our clothes at a big mall. Bats and balls can be bought at a sporting goods store. Hardware stores sell hammers, nails and other tools. You can go to a bookstore to buy your favorite book.

As the needs of the people in our community change, businesses *must* continue to provide new and different goods and services.

As we have learned, Clarkston has changed a great deal since 1823.

The people that live in Clarkston-Independence Township are proud of our lovely community. The old houses along Main Street are beautiful. We have many pretty lakes and parks.

You have a responsibility to take care of your community. We can help make it a clean, safe and beautiful place to live, work and play. *Clarkston's future depends on us.*